Contents

The Four Spheres

Scientists often look at Earth as a big system made up of several smaller systems called **spheres**. The nonliving parts of Earth's main system can be divided into three spheres: the hydrosphere (water), the geosphere (land), and the atmosphere (air). The living parts of Earth's main system make up the biosphere. These four spheres interact, or work with each other, to create balance and support life on Earth.

Earth is the only planet in our solar system known to support life. This means it's important for us to take care of it. To do this, we must first understand Earth's systems. This book takes an in-depth look at Earth's atmosphere—the gases surrounding our planet that protect us from the dangers of space and allow us to breathe.

System Connections

"Atmosphere" comes from the Greek words *atmos*, which means "vapor," and *sphaira*, which means "sphere." The atmosphere is the sphere of vapor, or air, that surrounds Earth.

Understanding Earth's Systems

Earth's Atmosphere

Melissa Raé Shofner

PowerKiDS press.
New York

Published in 2019 by The Rosen Publishing Group, Inc.
29 East 21st Street, New York, NY 10010

First Edition

Editor: Elizabeth Krajnik
Book Design: Rachel Rising

Photo Credits: Cover holbox/Shutterstock.com; pp. 1, 3, 4, 6, 8, 10, 12, 14, 16, 18, 20, 22, 24, 26, 28, 30, 31, 32 (background) Roman Sigaev/Shutterstock.com; p. 5 muratart/Shutterstock.com; p. 7 Micheal Aw/Lonely Planet Images/Getty Images; p. 9 De Agostini Picture Library/De Agostini/Getty Images; pp. 9, 11, 13, 19, 23, 29 (background) Ratthaphong Ekariyasap/Shutterstock.com; p. 10 24Novembers/Shutterstock.com; p. 11 Vasin Lee/Shutterstock.com; pp. 13, 14, 18, 20, 22 trgrowth/Shutterstock.com; p. 15 sashafolly/Shutterstock.com; p. 17 Chen Chien Hung/Shutterstock.com; p. 19 Paul Nicklen/National Geographic/Getty Images; p. 21 Kevin Key/Slworking/Moment/Getty Images; p. 23 V. Belov/Shutterstock.com; p. 25 LuckyVector/Shutterstock.com; p. 27 Vitoriano Junior/Shutterstock.com; p. 29 Anette Holmberg/Shutterstock.com; p. 30 Alena Brozova/Shutterstock.com.

Cataloging-in-Publication Data

Names: Shofner, Melissa Raé.
Title: Earth's atmosphere / Melissa Raé Shofner.
Description: New York : PowerKids Press, 2019. | Series: Understanding Earth's systems | Includes glossary and index.
Identifiers: LCCN ISBN 9781538329818 (pbk.) | ISBN 9781538329795 (library bound) | ISBN 9781538329825 (6 pack)
Subjects: LCSH: Atmosphere--Juvenile literature. | Earth (Planet)--Juvenile literature. | Meteorology--Juvenile literature. | Weather--Juvenile literature.
Classification: LCC QC863.5 S56 2019 | DDC 551.51--dc23

Manufactured in the United States of America

CPSIA Compliance Information: Batch #CS18PK: For Further Information contact Rosen Publishing, New York, New York at 1-800-237-9932

Without the atmosphere, life on Earth wouldn't exist.

Earth's Early Atmosphere

About 4.6 billion years ago, Earth began to form. It started out as a mixture of hot solids and gases with very little atmosphere. As the new planet cooled, volcanoes shot gases, such as methane and carbon dioxide, into the air. There was no oxygen in the atmosphere at this time.

After about 500 million years, Earth's surface was solid enough to hold water, and oceans formed. Chemical reactions in the oceans began to occur. **Molecules** containing carbon changed into living cells that could survive without oxygen. Around 2.7 billion years ago, the oceans became filled with tiny organisms called cyanobacteria, or blue-green algae. Cyanobacteria use a process called photosynthesis to make food and oxygen using carbon dioxide, water, and energy from the sun.

Through the process of photosynthesis, cyanobacteria began to add oxygen into Earth's atmosphere. Stromatolites, such as the ones pictured here, are fossilized deposits built by colonies of cyanobacteria.

System Connections

Throughout history, Earth's atmosphere has interacted with the biosphere. Life on Earth began as the atmosphere developed. Organisms began to **evolve**, which affected the development of the atmosphere. In turn, the changing atmosphere affected how organisms evolved.

Cyanobacteria and other simple organisms that used photosynthesis created a lot of oxygen. The methane in Earth's atmosphere reacted with this oxygen and, after about 2 billion years, the methane cleared. Oxygen levels in the atmosphere and the ocean greatly increased. For many early organisms, this was bad news: oxygen was poison to them and some species died out. This was called the great oxygenation event.

Some organisms in the oceans adapted to the higher oxygen levels. They used oxygen in the water to make energy. Evolution continued and, around 430 million years ago, life on Earth started to move out of the oceans. Tiny plants and **invertebrates** that could use oxygen directly from the atmosphere began to live on land.

System Connections

The great oxygenation event led to a huge increase in carbon dioxide (CO_2), a gas created when methane and oxygen combine. CO_2 couldn't keep Earth as warm as methane did, and the planet cooled and entered an ice age.

Plants use oxygen to break down the food they make during photosynthesis into usable energy. Plants also produce oxygen and release it into the air. Increased oxygen in the atmosphere helped plants thrive. By around 300 million years ago, they'd evolved to be huge.

Revealing Rocks

Scientists can learn about the atmosphere by studying the geosphere. When iron in soil and rock oxidizes, or combines with oxygen, it turns a rusty red color. These "redbeds" can tell scientists when the amount of oxygen in the atmosphere changed in the past. Some samples are more than 2 billion years old. Cathedral Rock in Sedona, Arizona, is a famous landmark made of redbed rock.

Something in the Air

Around 350 million years ago, about 20 percent of Earth's atmosphere was made up of oxygen. Oxygen levels continued to increase, and by around 300 million years ago, up to 35 percent of the atmosphere may have been oxygen. When Earth cooled about 250 million years ago and land plants died off, the atmosphere may have only been made up of about 12 percent oxygen.

The amount of oxygen in the atmosphere continues to change. Right now, it contains about 21 percent oxygen. The atmosphere contains other gases, too. About 78 percent is nitrogen, 0.93 percent is argon, and 0.4 percent is carbon dioxide. The remainder is a mix of small amounts of trace elements, such as neon, helium, and methane. The atmosphere may also contain **contaminants**, such as dust, ash, smoke, pollen, and toxic gases.

Many factors affect the composition of the atmosphere, including the weather, season, time of day, landscape, and location on Earth.

Where's the Air?

The atmosphere—often simply called air—is all around you all the time. It can't be seen, but it does take up space. An empty cube with sides measuring 2 feet (0.61 m) isn't empty at all. It actually contains 1.4 cubic feet (0.04 m^3) of oxygen, 5.2 cubic feet (0.15 m^3) of nitrogen, and 0.1 cubic feet (0.003 m^3) of other gases.

Keeping the Balance

The molecules in the air around Earth have a lot of energy. This makes them want to move up and away from the planet into space. Gravity, however, tries to pull these air molecules in toward the planet. The balance between gravity's pull and the energetic air molecules is what creates Earth's atmosphere.

The atmosphere is made of the same molecules throughout, but it's not just a single layer. It's actually divided into five layers, each with its own features. The layers work together to protect life on Earth from harmful things in space, such as meteors and solar **radiation**. They also keep the planet from becoming too hot or too cold. The atmosphere contains oxygen and carbon dioxide, which plants and animals need to survive.

Earth's atmosphere is about 6,210 miles (10,000 km) thick. However, this number isn't set in stone because there's no exact end to the atmosphere. Atmospheric gases in the air gradually **decrease** as you move farther away from Earth.

Climate Control

Earth has many climates, such as steamy rain forests, dry deserts, and icy polar areas, but they all have the same atmosphere in common. The atmosphere is constantly moving the hot air and cold air from various climates. This mixing creates storms, but it also keeps Earth's overall system stable by balancing oxygen levels around the planet and preventing any one part of the world from becoming too hot or too cold.

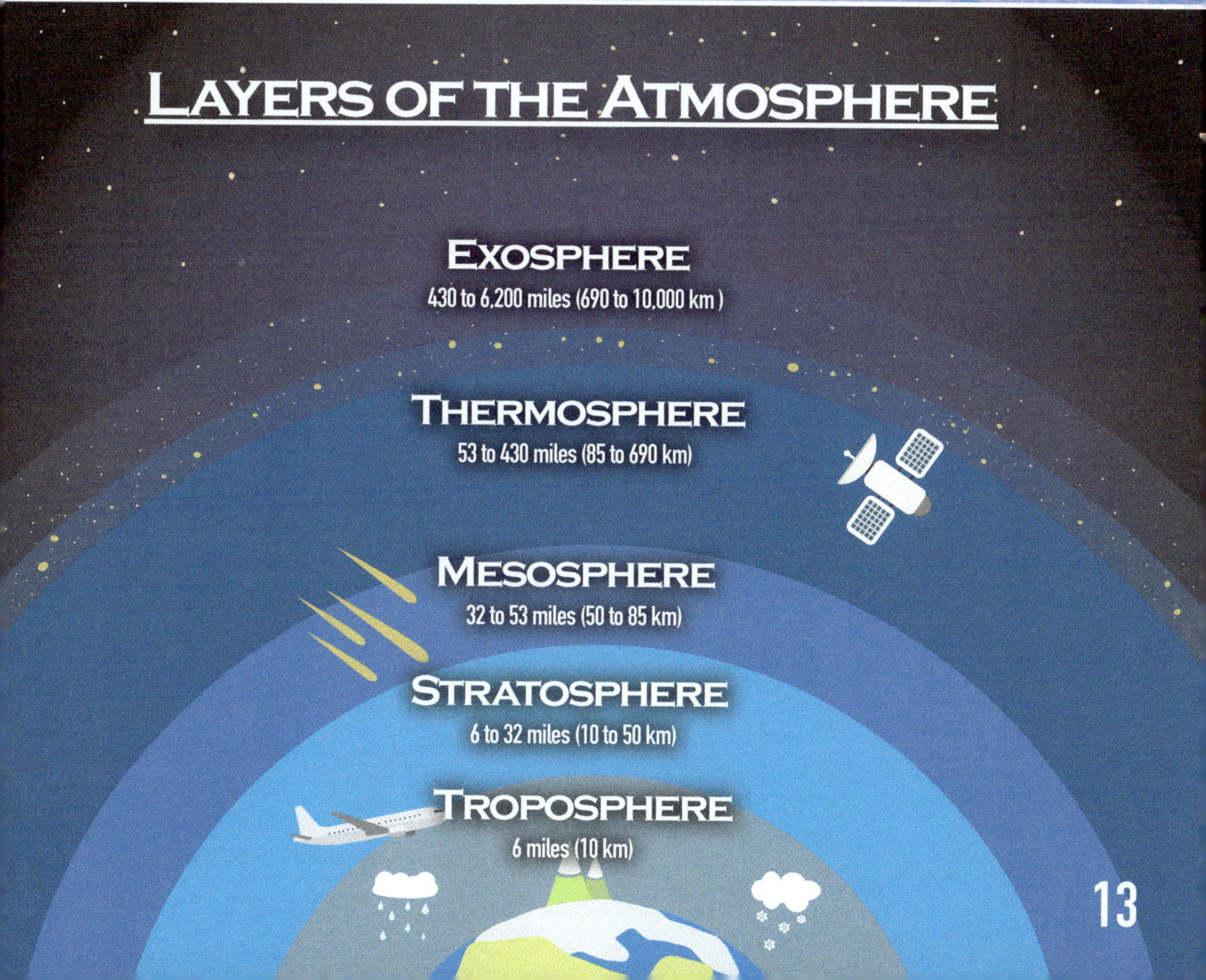

The Troposphere

The lower atmosphere is called the troposphere. This layer is closest to Earth's surface, and all life on Earth exists within it. The troposphere is between 6 and 10 miles (10 and 16 km) thick. This layer is greatly affected by Earth's surface, so the temperature varies. In places where it's colder, the troposphere is thinner.

The troposphere contains a lot of water vapor. When this water vapor cools, clouds form. Most of Earth's clouds form within the troposphere. It's also where Earth's weather occurs.

The upper boundary of the troposphere, which separates it from the next layer of the atmosphere, is called the tropopause. As you approach the tropopause, the temperature can drop as low as −103°Fahrenheit (−75°Celsius).

The troposphere is the only layer of the atmosphere where life on Earth can survive. It's where most of the atmosphere's oxygen is found.

System Connections

Air compresses under its own weight. This means about 75 percent of the atmosphere's mass is found in the lower 3.5 miles (5.6 km) of the troposphere.

The Weather Within

Weather is the daily state of the atmosphere, and it occurs mostly in the troposphere. Weather is made up of certain elements. When we think of weather, we most often think about precipitation and temperature. Water vapor creates precipitation, such as rain, snow, and hail, while temperature affects what type of precipitation forms.

Other elements of weather include wind, humidity, and atmospheric pressure. Wind is the movement of air across the surface of Earth. It occurs when rising warm air is replaced by cold air. Humidity is the amount of moisture in the atmosphere. Cold air holds less moisture than warm air. The weight of the air above a certain area is called atmospheric pressure. Scientists use atmospheric pressure to **predict** storms, which are **disturbances** in the atmosphere.

System Connections

The atmosphere is closely linked to the hydrosphere, which is all the water on Earth. In the water cycle, water moves between Earth and the atmosphere. The water changes from a vapor to precipitation and falls back to Earth, continuing the cycle.

The atmosphere traps energy from the sun, which changes the temperature of the water, land, and air near Earth's surface. These temperature changes create wind.

The Stratosphere

Above the lower atmosphere is the middle atmosphere, which contains two layers. The layer above the troposphere is called the stratosphere. The stratosphere reaches from the tropopause to the stratopause. The stratopause is the top boundary of the stratosphere, which is found about 32 miles (50 km) above Earth's surface.

Unlike the troposphere, the stratosphere gets warmer higher up. Topping out at around 32°Fahrenheit (0°Celsius), the temperature of the stratosphere is warm compared to some of the other layers of the atmosphere. This is because it contains the ozone layer, which is located about 14 miles (22 km) above Earth's surface. The ozone layer protects Earth's surface from huge amounts of dangerous solar radiation that can cause health problems, such as skin **cancer** and eye diseases.

Weather occurs in the troposphere, but scientists send weather balloons into the stratosphere. As the balloons float upward, their special instruments collect data about Earth's atmosphere.

The Ozone

The ozone layer is a natural part of the atmosphere. It's made up of a form of oxygen called ozone, which is a light blue gas that absorbs solar energy called ultraviolet (UV) radiation. Within the ozone layer, UV radiation is changed into another type of radiation called infrared, or IR, which heats up the stratosphere. Ozone is produced when electricity passes through the air, such as when lightning strikes.

The Mesosphere

The top layer of the middle atmosphere is called the mesosphere. The mesosphere and the stratosphere are separated by the stratopause. The top boundary of the mesosphere, called the mesopause, is between 32 and 53 miles (50 and 85 km) above the surface of Earth. The mesosphere has about the same percentage of oxygen, carbon dioxide, and nitrogen as the troposphere near Earth's surface. However, the air in the mesosphere is much less **dense** than the air in the troposphere.

The mesosphere is the coldest layer of the atmosphere. The parts closest to the mesopause can dip to temperatures as low as –130°Fahrenheit (–90°Celsius). Sometimes clouds of ice crystals will form even though there isn't much water vapor in this layer.

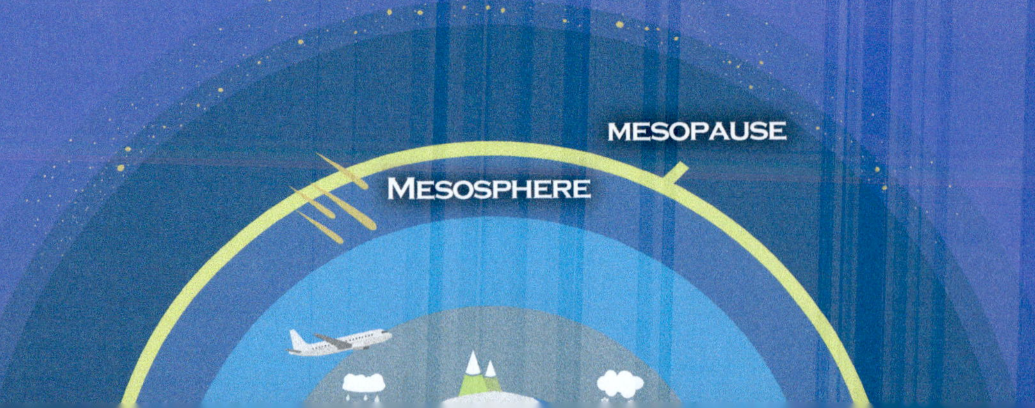

Even though it's so cold, the mesosphere is where objects from space, such as meteors, burn up. Traveling at tens of thousands of miles per hour, meteors hit the atmosphere, and the air in front of them quickly compresses. The compressed gases get very hot and burn the meteor until it's gone.

The Upper Atmosphere

Earth's upper atmosphere contains two layers: the thermosphere and the exosphere. The thermosphere begins at the top of the mesopause and reaches to about 430 miles (690 km) above Earth's surface. The air here is thin, but it absorbs a lot of solar radiation. The temperature ranges from 440 to 3,137°Fahrenheit (227 to 1,725°Celsius). The height of the thermosphere changes depending on how much solar activity there is. When energized particles in the thermosphere mix with particles from the sun, called solar wind, **auroras** can occur.

The exosphere is the outermost layer of Earth's atmosphere. Molecules here rarely run into each other because they are very spaced out. The exosphere reaches more than 6,200 miles (10,000 km) above Earth's surface. It's where space begins.

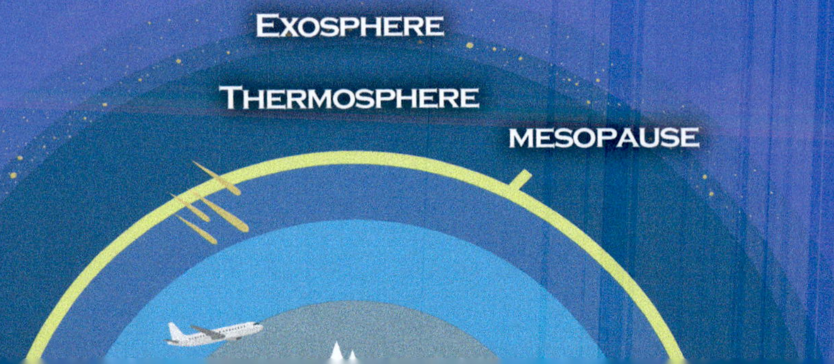

The place in the thermosphere where the ionosphere and magnetosphere overlap is where auroras happen. The aurora borealis, or northern lights, occurs in the Northern Hemisphere. The aurora australis, or southern lights, occurs in the Southern Hemisphere.

The Ionosphere and Magnetosphere

The ionosphere is part of the thermosphere. It contains many charged particles called ions, which form when solar radiation removes electrons from the gases in the atmosphere. The ionosphere can conduct electricity and affect radio signals. The upper part of the ionosphere is called the magnetosphere. The magnetosphere is filled with charged particles that are strongly affected by the sun and Earth's magnetic field.

Winds of the World

The atmosphere is filled with moving air. Global winds are the larger winds that move around the entire planet. Scientists describe these winds as cells, though you may have heard them called trade winds. Global winds are affected by temperature changes, differences in air pressure, and the spin of Earth on its axis. The way Earth's spin affects wind is called the Coriolis effect.

Wind carries gases and other particles through the air, sometimes for thousands of miles. The effects may be felt around the planet. For example, when a volcano in Indonesia erupted in 1815, ash and other tiny particles called aerosols were shot into the atmosphere. They blocked sunlight and caused temperatures to drop. It snowed in New England in June 1816 as a result.

The Coriolis effect causes winds south of the equator to spin in a clockwise direction, while winds north of the equator spin counterclockwise.

The Coriolis Effect

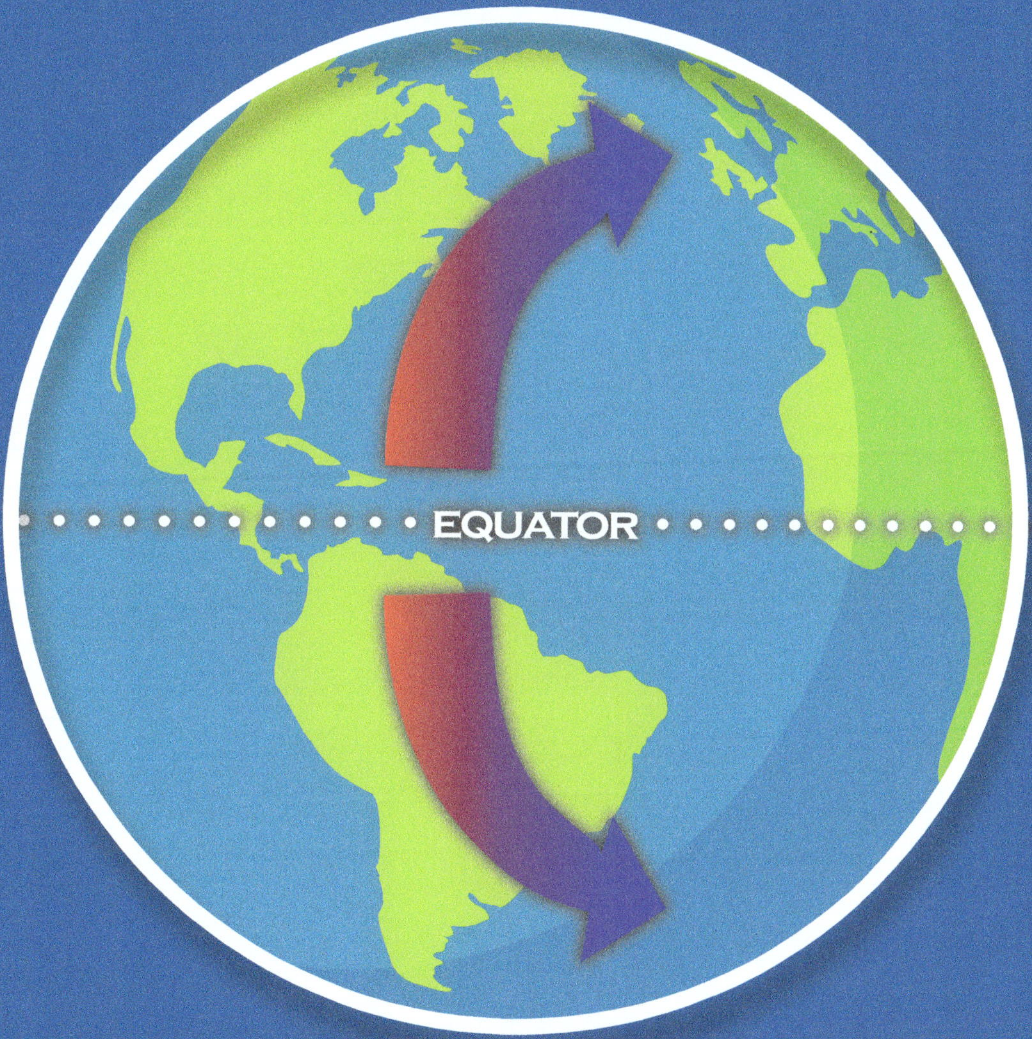

Greenhouse Gases

The atmosphere is sort of like a blanket for Earth. It keeps the planet warm by absorbing, or taking in, heat from the sun and trapping it inside. This process is called the greenhouse effect. Some of the gases that make up the atmosphere are called greenhouse gases because they're able to trap heat, like a greenhouse. Things in nature—such as decaying organisms, volcanoes, wetland areas, and bacteria—can create greenhouse gases. Factories and power plants, cars, livestock, and **fossil fuels** also create greenhouse gases.

Greenhouse gases are good because they keep Earth warm. However, if the planet gets too hot, terrible things can happen. As populations grow and human processes create more greenhouse gases, **global warming** is becoming a larger and larger problem.

During the day, some of the sun's energy enters Earth's atmosphere, while some bounces off the atmosphere, back into space. Most of the energy that enters the atmosphere escapes at night, but some remains trapped and warms the planet. →

System Connections

Chlorofluorocarbons, or CFCs, are chemicals once used in air conditioners, fire extinguishers, and spray cans. They stay in the atmosphere for a long time and are very bad for the ozone layer. Today, CFCs are banned in many countries.

The Greenhouse Effect

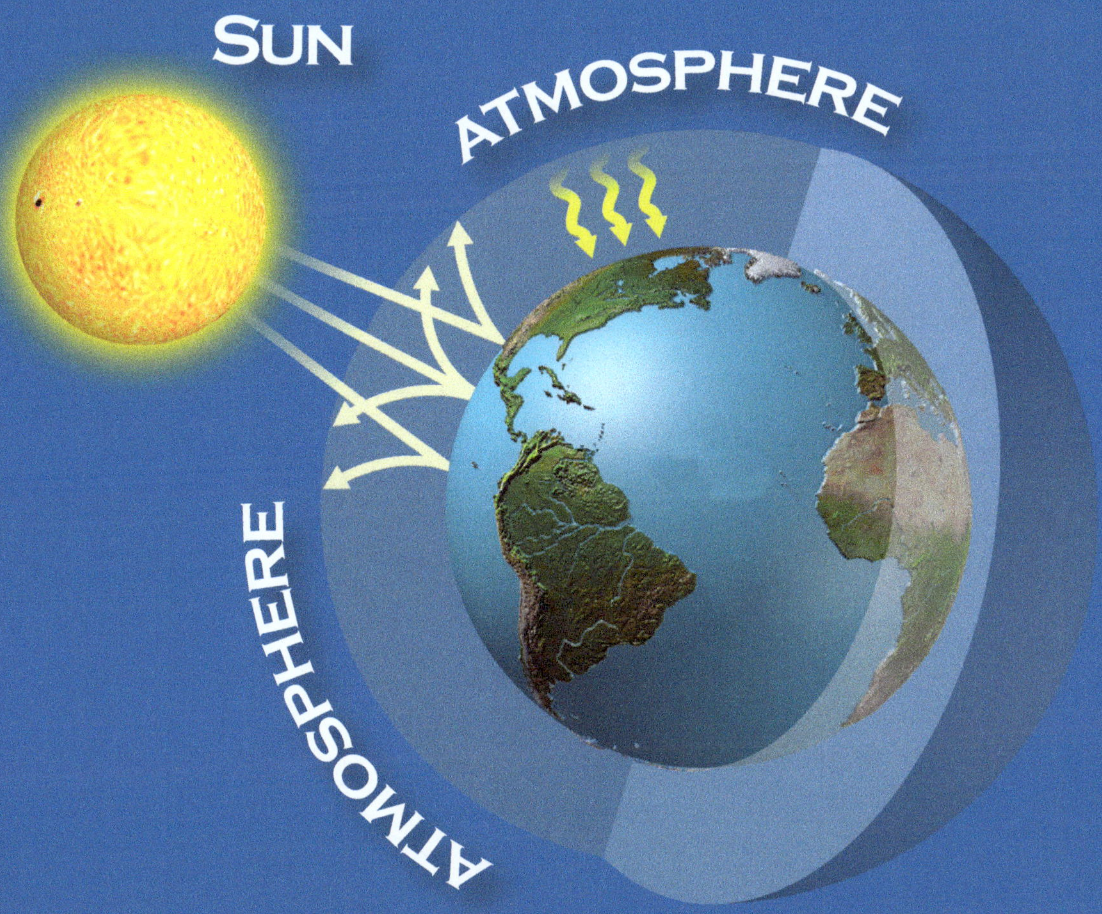

Global Warming

Scientists are worried that the burning of fossil fuels is releasing too much carbon dioxide into the lower atmosphere. People have also been clearing land to make room for growing populations. This means there are fewer plants and trees to remove carbon dioxide from the atmosphere. High levels of carbon dioxide mean more energy from the sun becomes trapped in Earth's atmosphere. This leads to a rise in air and ocean temperatures, which is known as global warming.

Global warming is already causing problems around the planet. Glaciers are melting, which is causing sea levels to rise. This puts populated coastal areas—such as Miami, Florida—at risk of serious flooding. Melting glaciers are also creating problems for animals, such as polar bears, that need the ice in order to reach their food sources.

An increase of one degree Fahrenheit in an individual location on Earth doesn't mean much. However, it means a lot when the global average temperature increases by one degree. Ice changes from a solid to a liquid with just a one-degree change.

Uh-Oh, Ozone

Ozone gas in the stratosphere is very helpful for protecting Earth from solar radiation. Unfortunately, ozone can also form closer to Earth's surface. There, it's considered air pollution, and it can make people sick. The amount of ozone increases when car exhaust mixes with sunlight. This is why big cities, such as Los Angeles, have higher levels of ozone and air pollution—and more people have health problems.

Saving the System

Earth's atmosphere is a very important system. Unfortunately, people have been harming it by burning fossil fuels and creating chlorofluorocarbons for many years. There's a hole in the ozone layer and global warming is becoming a bigger problem every day.

Scientists are learning more about how the atmosphere works. They are figuring out ways we can protect it. Banning CFCs has helped, but there's more we can do. Reducing our dependency on fossil fuels is the next step.

Without the atmosphere, life on Earth wouldn't be able to survive. It's also important to remember that the atmosphere is more than just an individual system. It's part of Earth as a whole. The atmosphere is closely connected to the hydrosphere, geosphere, and biosphere. By protecting our atmosphere, we're protecting all of Earth's systems.

Glossary

aurora: A natural display of colored arches of light that appear in the upper atmosphere.

cancer: A sickness in which cells multiply out of control and do not work properly.

contaminant: Something dangerous, dirty, or impure that pollutes a place or a substance.

decrease: To get smaller or less.

dense: Closely packed together.

disturbance: Something that bothers someone or something.

evolve: To grow and change over time.

fossil fuels: A fuel—such as coal, oil, or natural gas—that is formed in the earth from dead plants or animals.

global warming: A warming of Earth's atmosphere and oceans that is thought to be a result of air pollution from greenhouse gases.

invertebrate: An animal without a backbone.

molecule: The smallest possible amount of something that has all the characteristics of that thing.

predict: To guess what will happen in the future based on facts or knowledge.

radiation: Energy that comes from a source in the form of waves or rays you can't see.

sphere: An area of activity, existence, or authority. It also means an object shaped like a ball.

Index

Websites

Due to the changing nature of Internet links, PowerKids Press has developed an online list of websites related to the subject of this book. This site is updated regularly. Please use this link to access the list: www.powerkidslinks.com/ues/atmos